Amanda Chimera

Poems

Praise for *Amanda Chimera: Poems*

Inside every woman is another woman, a vanished twin, not so invisible as erased. We know her, don't we? The other self, the monster, who we hate to love. The sister. The mother. The Earth. The little girl we once were, the one who learned shame. *Amanda Chimera* has come to remind us that it is our life's work, loving her, letting go of the many forms of self-hate we inherit from others suffering the same. (Or, as the poet writes more elegantly, we must learn to *dream each other.*) In this wildly imagined and orchestral story, Mary B. Moore has given us more than a book of poems. *Amanda Chimera* joins the vital lineage of the region's Jungian writers like Gurney Norman, Joy Harjo, and George Ella Lyon. Here is a spiritually urgent myth, as delightful as it is fierce, ensuring Moore's place as an essential feminist poet of the Appalachian tradition.

—Rebecca Gayle Howell, author of *American Purgatory*

"Vertigo is her dance": combining classical erudition with a postmodern sensibility through the story of a twin who absorbed her dead sister's DNA in utero, Mary B. Moore explores the mysteries of identity, doubleness, agency, biological/generational destiny, botany, cryptozoology, and archetypal mythology as she brilliantly peels apart layers of consciousness and time. Her genius is polyphony—not just voice, but voices. "Beware. So many selves / nesting in the between."

—Claire Bateman, author of *Wonders of the Invisible World*

Amanda Chimera, Mary B. Moore's sixth collection, offers rich evidence of a poet who has come into her own. Using the duality of Amanda, and the "monstrous" ghost of her vanished twin, Gloria, Moore illuminates the shadowy corridors of personhood, individuality, and consciousness in language both incisive and frolicking. Whether writing about mysterious sisters, myth, family history, or issues of faith arising from her Catholic upbringing, Moore is a maestro of wordplay, and she brings this talent to bear in the multifaceted prisms of her poems. With painterly prowess, blazing intellect, and exacting attention to detail, she leads us, inexorably, to the realization that we are not monsters, but rather, reluctant custodians of our own vanished twin, "who isn't or might have been / or was."

—Frank Paino, author of *Dark Octaves*

In *Amanda Chimera*, Mary B. Moore addresses an unsettling truth—*something's inside her that's not her*. In poems composed of coursing blood, blue and red, the budding limbs of a fetus, a flower, a bird—the reader is introduced to Amanda and her vanished twin absorbed in utero, Gloria. We get to know these girls, their conflicts, their humor, and soon recognize—the faces of Amanda and Gloria are also faces of the speaker. A master of complex woven narratives, Moore contrasts the vanished twin fable with deep personal narratives and ekphrastic responses. We all have our monsters, our shadow selves and demon twins. The challenge of a lifetime is to fearlessly explore these entities, and Moore has done this brilliantly and bravely. I encourage you to read this book. *Let's welcome the new chimeras / who scour the abyss.*

—Robert Carr, author of *The Heavy of Human Clouds*

A search for wholeness that is more a celebration of the flawed, the broken, the incomplete. With deep empathy, surprise, and language rich and playful as Hopkins, Mary Moore's newest collection, *Amanda Chimera*, is a brilliant whiplash of a book that delights and challenges, each poem, "provoking you to love." And, wow, do I love this book!

—Lauren Slaughter, author of *Spectacle*

Also by Mary B. Moore:

Poetry Collections

Dear If, 2022
Flicker, 2016
The Book of Snow, 1998

Chapbooks

Amanda and the Man Soul, 2017
Eating the Light, 2016

Amanda Chimera

Poems

Mary B. Moore

MADVILLE
PUBLISHING

LAKE DALLAS, TEXAS

FIRST EDITION

Requests for permission to reprint or reuse material
from this work should be sent to:

Permissions
Madville Publishing
PO Box 358
Lake Dallas, TX 75065

Cover Design: Jacqueline and Kimberly Davis
Cover Art: Licensed through Adobe Stock
Author Photo: Tora Lavender

ISBN: 978-1-963695-05-2 paperback
978-1-963695-06-9 ebook
Library of Congress Control Number: 2024939289

To my daughter and husband,
who put up with joys and woes

Contents

Part 3

Part 4

"Vanished twin" refers to the absorption of cells and larger parts of a non-viable fetus by a viable twin during gestation. On rare occasions, the viable twin absorbs DNA in small quantities from the dead sibling, which accounts for the occasional discovery of two DNA profiles in a single person.

The monstrous body is pure culture. A construct and a projection, the monster exists only to be read; the monstrum is etymologically "that which reveals, that which [shows,] warns...."
—Jeffrey Jerome Cohen, *Monster Theory*

I like a mixed diction.
—Amanda

The Gone Twin, an Origin Myth

Though Mother played violin
to soothe the twins
swimming the amnios,
Amanda would play second
fiddle to no one.
She absorbed her twin,
spine still translucent,
arms still fins.
Or did Gloria sicken,
thin, and dissolve into Amanda's
cells, freckle her chin,
spot the right lung?

Amanda doesn't believe in
the Church God but imagines
Gloria is hidden
inside her like a soul. She'd sing

Glooow oh oh oh oh oh....
ohria in Excelsius De e o.
They'd duet, one low,
one high, a contralto
of sorts. Gloria
likes to jingle fast then slow
in Amanda's head as they go home
from Mom's salon, Bellisimo,

her cloth bag belling,
bracelets, earrings, pins.
Amanda wants to sing along,
a high quick flickering,
a vibrato; Gloria pings
like starlings
and chatters like monkey mind:
Amanda this, Amanda
that, how'd you get skin,
tongue, the body's bling?

Gloria's no saint.
Amanda is her haunt.

Part 1

Amanda Chimera

to Gloria, vanished twin

1
We rode lightless
the salt and soothe
of amnios,

two the egg-bellied
mother bore,
yoked twins;

we somersaulted,
bobbed and rocked
when the world walked,

pink sea horses,
eaters and swimmers,
footless dancers,
buds for limbs.

2
You died the Tuesday
Mother never knew you

drowned in the sea
of mother may I be.

Devolved,
cells and helices
fluid, you eeled

your way into me,
eye bud, ear hole,
heart's left chamber,

I your shroud and skin.

3
You weren't born
but I bear you.

Lonely only girl,
looking for kin,
I had gene-seers
read me, and *hello*,
they found you, lost twin
who spirals inside,
me and not me—

a star's arm, one-winged
bird, sole
spherule of pollen,
you're iffy as *suppose*—
a comma, a single parens, half
an iota.

We're gnomic, a riddle:
When is one, two,
two, one?
Which is you
when we're both also me?

4
You might have pitched
a mean curve ball,
long-legged runner
sprinting the grade-school bases,
sliding home
a "Hail Mary" hit.

Or we'd have lain face-up
on summer lawns,
finding heroes and animals
the night sky starred,
imagining our own:
the two sisters, the lyre,
the swan our swain.

You might have played piano
while I keyed the Mac,
our secret language a libretto

musical as Italian: all the words
end in *ah* or *ow* or *oh*,
the unworded sounds
of pleasure or loss.
Or we might be antonyms,
dissonance.

5
They tell me you'd
have been winged or hooved,
two-hearted,
one-eyed: a moon-calf.

I'm a chimera,
a zoo of two anyway.

My first lost half,
you haunt me
like Plato's myth of Eros:
he dreamed the envious
gods halved the first humans,
perfect spherical pearls
or moons,
to control their
unruly powers.

We still yearn
for our lost halves,
lean toward each other
across the abyss,
the difference.

6
You lived only
the womb-dream,
wisp of a wish, fiction,

who slipped
under my skin
alien
yet familiar,

an incarnation I
also am,
sister, demon, twin.

The Birds of Cutting

I'm tired today and blue to boot.
Nothing buoys me, yesses my no's.
Even the cardinal on the fence,
a dusky girl, isn't all red
like cardinal boys,
and the blue jays are goading
the white cat.
Fur spiked and matted,
he won't be hurried
or harried. Tail down, he slinks
finally under the porch.
The jays take off.
Like me, sometimes they're louts.

All the birds I notice
are red and blue, like blood—
blue in, red out.

The blue that shadows my eyes
agrees with the blue
veining my wrists:
in is better than *out.*

Red bolds its course,
is high-res, heady and heedless,
and the little mouths
I cut on my arm, bleeding and being
bled, hurt me into feeling,
a festival of hurt.

Look at my red letters:
read me, tell me I am.

Tuesdays in Amanda

Gloria is the undertow,
the underdour, though she too
sees the yellow pencils
of sunlight the blinds throw down,
the monarchs like leaves
fluttering the maple leaves,
but she hums the low
register of shadows
under the sofa,
of stones hunched in the garden.

It's Tuesday, bruiseday
when the blue patches
under Amanda's skin
go public. Gloria hums
a bumper car's electric engine,
then goes high pitched, a jet
working up crescendo,
and smacks Amanda's left
femur, careens off womb walls,
shudders the heart, stalls.

Gloria thinks Amanda's prismatic
in her teal blue taffeta
skirt, but prison isn't.
And metaphors
aren't windows or doors.
Buzz, buzz, she says: *hiss, thud.*

Amanda and the Man Soul

Amanda likes the mandolin's twang
and a good man. One's inside her,
says Jung. Her mantra
is *Amanda, Man, Amanda.*

She suns herself now
and listens to bluegrass
but can't forget the little man.
She is reading Jung.
She is not who you think she is.
She's just blackened her spiked hair
and bathes herself in aloe
to soothe the burn,
the fresh tats and arm cuts.

Amanda thinks the man lives in her chest.
She'd like to cut him out, but where would he go?
Jung says the man inside is her soul,
the sexes crossed. She's his hidey hole.

Amanda never hides.
The sun heats the book, her lap,
her jet-black hair. She'd like
a sturdy girl soul, thick knuckled,
chin squared, feet wide from working
the soil. She'd play mandolin's
moods, both lyric and bold,
but Amanda's stuck with the middle man
who taps in her chest like iambs.

The Vanishing Twin Does Vertigo

The window oak confettis
the light, and every iota
stutters

and whirls. It's Gloria.
She spins in the inner ear,
light-footed dervisher,

dervishing. She loves
the whirlies, the hover,
below becoming above, over

going under. But even pirouettes
lapse into done that's;
Gloria's got her limits.

She wears Amanda wearing a beret
and pencil skirt. She's her cachet
at the Sidewalk Cafe

where the litter has peaked
after lunch: a crow beaks
the green star on a cup, speaks

crow. He's green-blue-black up close,
like coal's petrol rainbows:
he's its official logo.

And the napkins, un-origamied,
not winged or domed,
are flimflam

the wind will gust.
The day's a kick or a bust
depending on how you adjust

the tilt, whether you're
the dizzier, the dizzied, or the blur
between, the Gloria factor.

The table's metal squares shed
a shadow, gridding
the sidewalk, rigid

cages and boundaries,
a quandary:
who's canary,

who's mine? Amanda can't hear
herself think. Gloria's rustling, bird
in a paper bag, weird

in the old sense—witchy.
She's an itch Amanda can't scratch.
Just when Amanda gets twitchy,

Gloria goes still, like the pause
between why and because,
act and applause.

Gloria's keen
to be heard, to be seen.
Vertigo is her dance.

Tremor Girl

drops the glass vase that
splatters
the tiles, types startle
for star, slips
the knife tip and bloods
the orange slices.

Her nerves jitterbug;
her left hand skips a key,
the right taps
a desk dance it didn't rehearse.

It's benign and familial, the doctors say,
the under-skitter.

She tremors like *terra unfirma*
where she grew up,
where earth can jostle
or shake you awake, teach
heart skip, breath catch,
adrenalin kick.

No wonder she lives
in the body of doubt.
She's the untoward, the awkward,
the missed
word. Her left eyelid
twitches; an elbow jerks.

Something's inside her
that's not her.

It's no one she knows,
dancer nobody

choreographs. Some nights,
as she's falling

into sleep, that delicious
swoon into not being

her, a low rolling stirs
under the bed:

an umber furred body turning
in its sleep, tidal

and almost gentle,
a brown bear, or it thunders

and shoulders rocks,
which rumble downslope,

percussion, repercussion:
earth music. She's the vibrato.

Antheraea Polyphemus

Mild-mannered mimic, its only defense, a lie,
the giant silk moth, named for Homer's cyclops,
bears eye-shaped spots its beige wings
flash. Threatened, it waves them
as if looks could kill:
think the variants: basilisk, peacock, Medusa.
Though dyeable, its silk doesn't sell:
the spun brown cocoon mimes its own
dry-river-loam look. Mouthless,
it mates and dies in a week: poor monstrous
brevity. Luckily it runs on auto, unconscious
we hope, its living death brought us
by the pheromone, Eros.

Hum for Gloria and Her Dream of the Same

Not her synonym
or homonym, you *ahem*
and *haw* at lunch, twitch Amanda's
right eye, hymn
the nearest icon, BVM
on a taco shell, Coca-Cola's flimflam
on the tube. You dummy up
new shrines and stumble
on the sacred in every idiom
fancy lights on. Fancy's the rummy
you met one Tuesday, unhomed
Homer: she fiddles and names
songs after the nameless,
the park's beheaded and disarmed
red oaks, beeches, elms.
Dread, Maim,
Calamity she calls them.
She even strums for the gone limb
you are. Fancy and you amp
into blues sometimes, or flame
a torch song in Amanda,
flicker some skit-skat, then disassemble
into smoke and mumble

like the mmmmm or om
you once heard at 4 a.m.
in Taos. Maybe it's atoms
whirring or Mom's
womb music, remembered:
you and Amanda, humming.

She Liked Ike, a Rhyme Bout

Mother was myopic but a crack
crossworder and picky
about which she worked,
preferring *The Times*—New York,
not L.A. She collected crossword topics
like the shapes of mandolin picks
in 16th C France, the history of the Picts,
and the names of dead but politic
prime ministers. She liked
words like *copacetic,*
philanderer, dysphoric.

She was freaked by black widows' knack
for hiding in boxes,
dog fur, cat dander, kinks
in the hose, snakes
of course, and the Moby Dick
of cockroaches she imagined lurking
under the stove. Luckily,
there was Gentleman Jack.

Though she bickers
with me even now and snickers
at my writings, she secretly likes
me tapping away on my Mac.
Words like *balalaika,*
played with a twang and a flick,
click Mom's Bic,
though she'll deny it with a trick
of her lip and a run of tongue clicks
and *tsks.*

Camera Head

Dad liked gambling, the trifecta, *oh*
and awe, the jockeys' turquoise

and neon pink, hullabaloo
and photo finish,

his heart beating and lifting, red hope
he rode. His eye apple, show

girl at Pimlico,
I was risky: I might pose

good girl, or pucker o's,
or guffaw. He photoed me

black and white, kodachromed me,
tinted me sepia. Poseur.

I loved the two-holed
double-lens reflex, flat-nosed,

box-headed, square window
where brains should be stowed.

He let me see it arc, bow,
distort even him. And from no,

from blank, in the red-lit shadows
the darkroom brewed,

silver vowed to light, and now
me, now my mother, then a sunflower

fully blown, large brown
eye like a doe's.

Eyeing and eyed, we photo-troped
between is and pose.

Morpho Didius

Wings pinned open to pose
the lie of flying,
they out-blue sky.

But that's disguise:
pigmentless, refraction
is their hue, cells

attuned to blue. And see,
they're perfectly preserved,
soul symbols, a pair of them,

boxed under glass for eternity.
The wings iridesce
royal blue, turquoise,

periwinkle: blue boys,
more collectible
than dullard girls.

Their kin no doubt adorned
eighteenth-century
curiosity cabinets, catchalls

for colonial finds:
rhinoceros horns attributed
to unicorns, mandrake roots

forked like men, shells
shaped like ears, tumors with hair.
Today we embalm the once alive

in formaldehyde's acrid
soul-colored fluid
or box them in a vacuum

like these. They prove Camus
was right: death alone halts
metamorphosis.

The Morphos' pose,
perfect for blue's boast,
hides the underwings'

sweet eye spots, *ocelli*,
evoking *uccello*,
the Italian bird, though these

lack a song. The blind
undereyes awe
beauty's predators.

Imagine, lying face-up
on the ordinary evening
lawn, as flocks of Morphos

migrate over, the sky's
blue not quite
disguising the celestial

ocelli flashing, as if sky
were million eyed.

Part 2

Ab Ovum

I could say anything's inside me, Gloria, Dad, Mom,
the old Royal typewriter, Xs, Ys, a blue '58 Hudson . . .
but I Wiki-checked the car and learn they quit making them
in '57 so then I wonder if I mean the Hudson River,
which is miles wide some places like the Great Lakes
it led Hudson to—that's a lie—Erie wasn't canalled yet—
but I don't feel like researching it.
I could say little old ladies spin in a long corridor
inside me, but their names are Greek and while euphonious,
hard to remember—Is Mnemonic one?
Maybe I should word only stuff I know,
the ridge that droops like an old
work horse's sway back, which
I see every time I look out my window,
and it's wooded and generous,
forming this green hammock the sky
lolls in, where clouds burgeon and droop
or sail or gallop, and it also curves
like a lopsided smile,
but smiling is a bit trivial to be inside me.
I'd prefer Shakespeare and the Pacific
all tragicomic, scintillating
with little stars, asterisks of refraction,
and a Mariana Trench
of profundity—speak it, and here it is.
So many things are inside me
I could start again anywhere,
like that small ultramarine horse ornament
I've saved for years, its saddle beaded red, green, and yellow,
stuffed with feathers or hair, I wonder whose?
Maybe my Irish grandmother's,
the one I never met, who Dad said
sang Vaudeville before
a client stabbed her to death
with an icepick, which a Chicago newspaper
c. 1933 verified, and whose image
no photo shows because
Dad never had one and he's gone now anyway.
Now I did go *ab ovum*—candled

Grandmother's empty cameo,
origin's luminous wind-egg.
No wonder I've swallowed all
the words—to fill the harrow and hollow.

Amanda and the News, c. 2016

Listen: it's that *chew chew chew* bird—
hungry for pencil ends as he contemplates
the next phrase, or it's been-there,
eaten-that bird who ruminates
the walnut leaves' crinkle and curl,

their too-bright green, their new.
Does he know he's new?
I'm old as stones and not as solid.
Gloria fritters a while
and fiddles my left eardrum,

a tickle not a hum. See the redbud?
She thinks that's her, the flesh-bud
that never flowered. The President on CNN
says he'll send the babies
he's caged to asylum cities for spite.

Gloria aches under my ribs.
Later we pause and watch another
window where blouses, jeans,
and undies wash. Crumpled like wishes,
they form a loose ring, turning.

She gets the whirlies; I'm just mesmerized
or is it mercerized? Have mercy
on us, Blessed Mary, I used
to pray. I still like her white and blue,
sky's wardrobe, the sea's. I think

I'll pour a chardonnay. I'm old like slate
and due for erasure. "Sweet Baby Jebus,"
we saw once, spray-painted on an overpass,
uncage those babies. I'd pray if I thought
a god, a mercy, could hear.

Gloria, Arbored

Gloria would like to be
not-Amanda, but she needs
an outside to be inside.
Maybe Juno would
arbor her in the three-boled juniper
near the porch, or is it
already three sisters, braided?
Juniper means *ever young*,
though its bark, fissured
and grooved, scaled in spots,
looks ancient, saurian, piscine.

The foliage simmers or shivers,
airs itself out, and the round
leaf-scales, which join and branch,
make each stem a flat little tree:
a tree of trees.

Air breaches and touches
the juniper everywhere.
And in its blue-green torch shape,
narrowed at the top,
its foliage almost a spiral,
Gloria could feel
how ascending so far
is drinking air
is dwindling infinitely into it,
and thirst is rooting beneath.

But the red oak in the park would also
suit her. Four-boled, sororal,
the bark blushes dusk rose
or mauve where it's furrowed.
Here she won't dwindle
but spread, bare each wide
two-skinned leaf-self to air:

multitudes, skewed everywhichway,
so many selves,

tethered, still
sistered and mothered.

Blazon, "Figure of a Winged Monster"

from Ambroise Paré's *On Monsters and Marvels*, 1573

The single ladylike horn curving up
from the fontanelle, the sculptural
curls and aquiline nose
mimic Greek art's symmetries.
Even the wings emerge smoothly
where arms would bud,
their extension drawing her breasts up, out:
a trick the artist learned in the atelier?
The torso's musculature
is closely observed: art or anatomy
or both sired her and the vulva
and penis side by side below
the belly's slight feminine bulge.
Fish and mermaid scales,
musically arranged in
decrescendo, sheathe
and adorn her lower
body, but fins aren't her finale.

One eye peers out where knees
would be, and she's pedestaled
on a four-toed bird foot,
rendered realistically, well clawed.
What would the lower eye see or
foresee? Maybe she has third sight.

Did the artist draw her
for a laugh, a dare?
Poor monster, Shakespeare's Viola
said of herself.

Maybe Ravenna's hybrid
is God's bird-footed bride?
Or is she herself the god,
or a hymn, embodied,

26

all the creatures
that Earth engenders, one
sacred polyphony?

Light Lures

Sand flies of light
leap and glint on the beach,
likeable from a distance.

In the deep trenches
spectral jellyfish luminesce,
their see-though bodies
fluid as ectoplasm,

and now that cameras are built
to sustain the monstrous pressure
of sight in the benthic depths,
we can watch for the first time
anglerfish sporting light lures
in the otherwise lampless place.
They're conveniently set
over rows of teeth, wide
as Carroll's cheshire-cat grin.
Their jaws, loosely hinged,
swallow amplitude, awe.

Let's welcome the new chimeras
who scour the abyss.
Luciferin's the chemical
that lights its photophores blue.

Amanda, Beached Like the Sand

Dillon Beach, California

These sheer gelatinous disks evoke
the urge to poke, but Amanda
inspects them only by eye. Almost
transparent, wider than her foot,
their *in* and *out* are all one:
even the plumbing shows.
Their organs ordered by fours,
sacs like stomachs, wombs,
hearts, essential and
usefully redundant,
are joined by pipes
in the same unassuming gray.
No inward mystery here.

She avoids stepping on them
though they aren't the same vivid stuff
as her. Senseless, since eyeless,
whiskerless, and noseless,
they must be imperiled,
feeling their way through the knowing
waters—maybe they're all
feeling, without wiles—
unless senses unlike ours imbue
the lachrymose jell.

Whatever their powers,
medicinal or venomous,
she needn't collect them;
they're best left here, beached
like the sand. Despite
their idiosyncratic concentric style,
even the gulls, those delecticians
of shore orts, shark chum,
and whale gut, ignore them.

Here: she can see the sand
through one, an alien lens,
the grains magnified,
queerer, more opaque.

Amanda as the Saint of Red

The saint of red wears
only rose-gold halos
and braids her Orphan-
Annie hair
spider-leg thin, snaky,
a challenge
she binges mornings on.
If she mirrors
too long, she'll stone herself
like Medusa;
no whirling then,
no dervishing or girling.

Best text home, or sew
red buttons on blue blouses,
or listen to music,
not the blues
but razzmatazz gospel music.
She gets high
on a full-throated soprano.

If you count the buzz
she steals from bees,
redbud and fireweed,
which all undeaden
the park this spring,
she's a bloody stoner.
Aren't all saints?

She's like the carnations
she loves
the incarnadine of—
never quite buttoned up.
Circles of ruffle-lips,
they'll tickle your face
if you bend too close,
unrepentant.

In the shower, she hums
Te Deum riffs
and lauds her god who's
awe, or is it dread?

Amaryllis Belladonna

We didn't plant them but they rise
anyway, pink trumpets,
two, three, four per stem, sisters.

They'd trill if they could:
naked ladies, we called them as kids.
Leafless, the blooms dilate,

stamen, ovum—*come-on*
all shown. Did their display
tempt my neighbor to his?

He's arrested and not for a camera's
exposure, his penis a pink
microphone. Maybe it beseeches

alone and untouchable to go—
See me, it says, *I am.*
When I was seven, a man showed me his

from a car door. Its tip oozed,
red and swollen. Gloria
thought it was sick or angry.

I ran home so fast I scraped
one knee on the steps.
That week I made flower art with

crepe paper and pinking shears—
which cut little teeth or frills.
Gloria hidden,

I made Mom, Dad, cat—each
edged like gears, the family
a machine for not telling,

each alone, affectless.
But the amaryllis go pink
and trill, buck-naked,

lean and loll to and fro,
sisters, familial
air sharers, the petals'

notched edges geared
to air, the risks and powers
of self-exposure, shared.

In the Dress of Mirrors

The window enters through her eyes,
the same window that changes the trees
and deranges them each day
like thoughts, finches that flit and
tousle her hair. This involves
a new grammar: the vertigo at the stairs' top
will loll in her calves; *hello* and *farewell*
stammer on her tongue; and the urge to walk out
of the room, the life, itches at her heels
like wing buds. You want to slip your thoughts
into the rooms of her, flex with the leaf light
at the glass, be the rising notes she
queries when the doorbell rings:
who's there? But she's opaque in her quicksilver
dress and will not let you see in.

Amanda Penelope

I jiggle one knee because
I always do. The larkspurs,
improbably blue, nod out the window,
and further afield,
purple thistle and cow parsley
like hand-crocheted doilies,
also called Queen Anne's lace.
They all agree with some claim
I can't hear the shadows make
or the sun or the eucalyptus.

My sister, who isn't or might have been
or was, comes out the door.
She's a sleeve and a collar, a sideview
of a brow. I'm not alone or I am
daydreaming Penelope
though I never wove
except once when I walked from bar
to car, which luckily stalled.

I hope something besides *want*
emerges from the field.
The flowers and tall grasses sway now—
the wind sheers across it,
a sail, passing. It's not Odysseus,
nor my sister. (Odd
how they almost rhyme.)
It must be the weather's fore-hem,
the skirt of the impending.

I knit today, each stitch
a promise, knit and purl,
knit and purr: its rhythm
mesmerizes, I breathe it.

The needles click the brittle
talk of beetles and grasses,
the field brewing flowers
named after animals,

itches, and queens.
Waiting is not my bane.
There, I just dropped a stitch
and found it again. Morning
is my only paramour.

To the Miscarried Child

On Van Gogh's *Irises* at Arles

The irises aren't eyed, but tongued:
the three bearded sepals
droop, pant, loll

among the splayed jade-green blades,
while behind the jumbled
tilted flowers,

a bird's head buds,
its two white eye spots
eyeing us: hybrid,

half-plant, half-animal,
like the foam-formed
almost human shapes we imagine

Turner's turbulent seas cast up—
Poseidon, or something stymied,
unable quite to be,

like you, like me,
ma soeur, ma semblable.
A few buds ape the brush's shape,

fuse art and artist.
The one white iris
tugs us into its cup,

outlier among the blues,
poor blind boast.
We think white looks

like absence not plenitude
though it's all colors married.
And you, dear jilted ghost

of *almost*, veined iris-blue
in the dark womb water,
still porous, a skein,

all eyelets and mouths,
gone before you'd grown
the human husk:

if you'd had the luck
to be born,
would Vincent's irises

have awed you too?
The terrors his brush disclosed,
bad gods among the beauties.

On the Meme of the Irish Mermaid Li Ban

We cannot know how the sea cradled
and buoyed her. In the meme, she stands

in the ether's tide, woman-fish, arms spread,
almost a Medieval manuscript's

illuminated T. Stylized diamonds
mark sea and sky like the sun nets

I've seen skein the Pacific:
the swells pulse under them,

muscular like a swimmer's
back as she reaches and pulls.

Dad steered and held me as a girl,
the old photos show, taught my feet

and arms to mimic swim and float.
I imagined mermaid-me

sheathed in scales, gill-less
and guileless—able to breathe the sea.

But the land-serpent, River Flood,
swallowed Li Ban's father.

Was it grief that remade her a sea maid?
She swam the tear-colored ocean, dove

and leaped the weirs, slipped the nets
pursed between animal-skin boats.

Men's myths say she acted
the siren, the Lorelei,

until some monks net, revise,
and saint her.

In the Twitter-sphere,
she's still sea creature or goddess,

her hair a school of curls
like the arcs, crescents, and whorls

certain Irish stones bear—
inscrutable lunar alphabet.

Her eyes all pupil, belly
oddly rounded, and the navel,

a third eye: does she bear a vision,
or the snake ouroboros,

a living hoop, an O or howl
the finned woman sings?

Isn't her siren call
mourning, not luring?

Part 3

What the Rosary Beads Say

They're matte and wooden,
pot-iron black, but not mute:
coiled in a pewter jar,
they click and gossip, parochial-
school nuns, nodding heads.
His mother was not a good woman
he told me. *Tsk tsk*, says the rosary.
Duller than coal, the tarnished
droop-necked Christ, nailed
to Torture's metal T.
The beads rattle like pebbles
at the well's bottom.
I fall into it when I open the jar:
tarnish and musk, prayer bones,
wooden tears, seeds.

Van Gogh's Howl

On *Cypresses*

The brushwork sinews the trees'
dark green, the paint so thick,
even the museum postcard
shows the strokes horn in and out,
finger each other.
Each is almost a figure.
The yellow crescent moon,
half a mouth, howls:
the paint burls around it,
a series of inset lips, a rose.

I howled once, fled
the house at two a.m.,
not where cypresses
line the great vineyards' drives,
but under November sycamores
near the SP tracks: I ran,
stumbled, almost fell, and
ran again, ripped my shirt,
and stretched my lips
so wide the wordless
vowels hurt. And nobody heard,
saw, or dared to.

In the painting, nobody's face,
or mine or yours, surfaces
in the fore-tree's bark,
eyes and mouth round,
lit beige: has a god arbored
another woman—tongueless
but not senseless—to feel,
bleed, die in that body
only partly wood?

Here and there, a touch
of emerald and beeswax gold
lights on the foliage;

and the delta of sky
between the two trees,
arced strokes, over-rippling
coils or concentric petals hover:
not serpentine, but floral,
a blue rose. Heaven
is burls, howls, roses.
The cypresses writhe.

Saviors

Crucifixion fresco, chapel, Castello di Postignano, Umbria

1
In my too-American dream,
Hell's Angels and their Harleys
roar by even here, on the Umbrian hills,
startling Gloria and the three
village dogs,
some sheep, and one llama
whose aristocratic head and neck
form an upside-down J
for jail or Jesus.

2
The Medievals who liked to wall in
older walls hid the fresco,
but earthquake laid it bare:

the fore-wall's pink-gold stones,
abraded and spalled,
tumbled and formed a jagged arc
under Christ's feet.

The restorers left the wall
to frame him in the ruin.

3
Augustine called the way Eros
weighs down our torsos and thighs,
that gravitation earthward,
pondus amoris, love's weight.

In crucifixion, the Roman
engineers pitted it against Christ.

4
Father, stroked nearly
mute since I was twelve,
who couldn't think, work, drive,

a bastard whose favorite curse word
was bastard, drives the narrow
winding roads to rescue me in the dream,
his cotton-candy pink
Nash Metro veering
around the bends.

His slippers slap the asphalt
when he stops—shuffle,
stutter, the invalid's
rhythm, the incompetent's—

but his pink chariot
carries me off:
addle-headed savior.

5
And Christ, poor bastard,
his dad an absence,
hangs there nailed
to the damned cross,
showing his scrawny sixpack,
the one knee bent back like a starlet's.
He doesn't even need his dad:
he could have soared—
god-dragon, blue angel.
And this is the mystery—
his hands and feet bored through,
he stayed, he suffered the crowd roar,
the spitting and fisticuffs
among the riffraff
whose savior he believed he was.

6
In Postignano's fresco, no crowd
gathers. Each figure is isolate.
Even the Virgin looks away.
So does the righthand angel,
cloaked rose, the left one, in green.
Their robes billow:
they ride divinity's transparent

medium. Maybe the Medieval
artist could manage only one register
for faces, a sweet blankness,
angels, saints, Virgin, all akin
in indifference or
innocence.
Even the walls are sanguine.

Embroidering

She faces the blank sky of New Jersey,
white and gray. She cannot find a mood,
a key for being Amanda
when the seeing is so dank:
she settles in lamplight's pool
to do some crewel, so bored
is she, so uncool; draws
in dresser's chalk
a pool of ruffles, a skirt,
and fits it out with a girl,
ponytailed, pigeon-toed.

Amanda lacks the gene
for nicey-nice
but works her stitches like a pro:
French knots dot the eyes;
herringbone feathers
the tail; rows of chain batten down
the satin-stitch ruffles.

She likes the one-sided girl,
the tail grown sideways
from her head, a chimera of sorts,
like a horse with arms.

But on the verso, a chaos
of stitches, knots, zigzags,
turns, reversals,
a synapse map—Gloria's
work. Amanda flutters
her hindmost wings and sighs:
Amanda embroiders Amanda.

Wound and Ground

Aunt's painting of an Asian sage

Lao-Tzu, Confucius, we don't know who,
rides an ivory ox. Gold and green checks

robe him like sun-dappled lawn.
Maroon-red or umber grounds him

and maybe mimics the living room's
wound-brown mahogany. The chairs' curved legs,

bird claws grasping each foot,
lumbered the rugs and furnished

her nightmares when one day she was told
she is not who she was: not sister, daughter,

but sister's daughter, a lie lied to, a bastard.
The word haloed every boundary, every

afterwards. The lyre-back chairs' lemon-wax glow
ached behind the eyes; the chinoiserie

vases stuttered, shimmered; and the sage wore
migraine's aura or lens, the sacred

made sensible as pain.
The bastard knowledge is holy.

Maybe painting the ox's muscular shoulders
helped her bear being born

again, and the sage's robe, the checks'
yin and yang flags, unflagging

complements, were brief
gaiety, and still flicker, unchecked

against the lie's slow bleed.

Gloria, as the Jilted Girl

Grays and grim yellows suit her. She's a mood,
like light on a leaf-muddled pond.
The umber of cattails, swaying
against each other, shadows her hair,
two large braids turned like seashells
at each ear. Juniper berries green
her eyes, their transparency, gin's.
No wonder she wanders the ledges
of ponds and windows, halts near thresholds
and doorsills, at ease in liminal
places like the angels in Renaissance
paintings, aloft in corners, mostly eyes and wings.
She can wash you in feeling, which is all
she is now—having disavowed breath—
and hovers at your edges, weightless as vows.

Wings

In the walls, a flurry: maybe
miniscule cherubs, rose cheeked,
working their wings.
They derived—did you know?—
from winged skulls, angelic
death's heads.

More likely bees or wasps
fly in the between, where the joists
join the rafters—
joys nailed to raptures,
or not.

Wing buzz atonal,
they fly, eat, groom
among the two-by-fours,
wolf spiders, and ants;
the wasps build papier maché pipe organs
and the bees, a wax dome
that the queen, astute by gene,
occupies. Ivory colored and larval,
her body's all ovary.

Maybe the house's history
invites them—we two at home
with the imaginary.

Do they get winded, wings so busy?
Wind almost *wings* anyway,
a typo like *love* and *live*.

Lavish, the filigree
their genes tat the wings with, thread
and space, is and isn't.

The wing buzz quiets at dusk.
Or maybe I imagine it,
the bees and wasps of me—

stingered too.
Beware. So many selves
nesting in the between.

Speaking the Beast

The manticore's man head bares a shark's three
rows of teeth, his carnivore creds, befitting the lion body,

but what god arked him and the real lions,
the egrets, housecats, and butterflies?

Man-born, imagined like the giant cyclops,
this beast's all maw. Maybe a fantasist doodled

it on a manuscript's foot, an apt
caricature, the abbot in a snit,

or a Renaissance travel writer
nightmared it up after imbibing a foreign

herb. The hero who kills it
wreathes himself in myth

and dons a necklace of teeth—
as if the beast had swallowed him

headfirst. Neck tingling with the jaws'
remembered force on the spear's iron haft,

wearing the mouth he's reborn from,
he's heeded whenever

he speaks the beast,
boasts he bested and ghosted it.

After he inks it, the monk is rapt.
What splendor and horror

can be thought.

Deflections

The veils barely inured me
to sight, so mirroring

became how I deflected looks.
I bore reflection the way

the pond bears the fir trees
and clouds:

the water's skin
is shift and to and fro;

it rubs the earthen
and celestial together,

blurring boundaries.
Maybe my father had looked

too much, a thumbing
without touching,

a hunger, an incursion.
(Please don't look.)

I wear my mutable
dress again, the mirror-

colored rain's
dazzle and blur,

its flexible strands.
The rain rises too as fog,

various pale
flowers—orchid, mum,

the white-green
hydrangea—a veil

of whorls almost erasing
mirror's fragile witness.

Gloria Knows What Amanda Knows

and shadows her dream-
dancing, though which is the *her*
she is confuses Gloria's every move.

Now she crooks to look like
the letter K, one leg, one arm out;
then she stoops to humped woman,

heedless and headless; or bends,
bare poplar the wind plays:
skeleton, crazy-sticks, jangle girl.

In one dream, she's grace,
long-necked bird girl, water-borne,
a swan on the prow.

Sometimes, she's fleet
light skimming the bay.
Amanda eyes the cormorants

swimming, moveable round heads
the bay's lisp and lapse washes.
They stand on the pier

and spread their wings to dry, dark
avian crosses. Amanda wakes
to heart lift, breath swell—a sense

she's on the verge, at the stairs'
top, the bay's edge. She balances
the urge to fly or fall

against the pulse's impulse to be
two: beat, pause; in, out; her, her.

Amanda, Showing the Father

1
My father Dominic Loewe
used to say when I sassed he'd lower
the boom if I were
his daughter, then he'd remember
I was, and Gloria
too, though he didn't know her,
and he'd pour himself a whiskey sour,
wish-key to the door
of a restored Anaheim where
the orange groves' crowns,
the boles that tree-moss powdered
poster-paint green, were
still a power, like the neon tower
at the movie theater, Lowe's—
no relation. Drunk, his own crower,
he'd say his sales made Cutter Lab's soar
until the bad vaccine. He dowered
me with sample boxes, small cardboard
houses. I made streets, neighborhoods, towns
where fathers were neither senile nor dour.

2
On summer weekends,
his penis peeped out
his boxers. One-eyed
voyeur, flabby finger
his thigh grew, do-nothing,
malingerer,
flute with only one hole:

what was it for?
Did he show it on purpose?

Gloria was very quiet.

A whale couldn't pass through it,
or a yellow school bus,
a girl in blue-and-white-checked uniform skirt,

a Coors can,
the White House,
Ike,
the squadrons of WWII fighter planes Dad flew in
and watched with me in *Victory at Sea*,
nor of course the *Enola Gay*,
nor the dark red roses with peppery nose he
grew for my mother.

You see, I cannot
look at the thing itself,
though familiar
as Old Golds, Pall Malls,
the O'Keefe and Merritt stove,
but must clothe it
in metonymy, hyperbole—

3
When I finally saw a man's erect
I didn't imagine my father's.

I felt its moveable skin,
silk on a pipe,

saw the dew beading
the flute hole, a one-

note song I wasn't
ready to play:

I was a child's glove,
too tight a fit,

and whetted, the boy burned
and tore as he thumbed inward,

and feeling something akin
to love, moved at first gently.

4
Dad's last resort was Journey's End
Trailer Park. He planted the yellow roses
Mom and Gloria loved.
Lucky he landed in Santa Rosa
where no tornados thumb down,
bully and flatten trailers like roadkill.
Dad didn't blow away but Pall-Malled
himself out: the gorgeous

red packs gorgoned him:
smoke rings snaked around his head,
braiding and unbraiding, spirals
and half-curls. But his bachelor-button
blue eyes stunned no one
into stone. Later, I'd gin up
my own catatonic tonic.

5
Some nights we star-fished:
Pisces, the Big Dipper, Orion
whose sword pointed always
Earthward: Stories rode the night sky.
And I, his little starlet:
he won a prize for me
at five, photographed
while bathing, hair
piled on my head, a dark crown.

6
I remember no trespass,
no blush heating my face:
I thought everyone's
father showed.

7
Gloria imagined the innocents,
our fore-children,

huddled in the breast-shaped huts,
earth's mud and straw teats,

fire embering the center,
smoke rising through the blowhole

at the top, and the children
at two, six, twelve

witnessing the four-legged,
four-armed animal

moan, lift, and fall,
riding being ridden.

The child fur would rise
on their arms, and they'd hide

their eyes, the monster—
or was it a god?—so awed them.

8
Blameless as our father's
baby-blue eyes, I saw
only a wrinkled one-eyed thing,
cyclops, no seer

or power or wand,
a useless finger, pipe
without a song,

nothing I needed,
nothing at all.

Part 4

Bike for Two During the Sequestration

Ritter Park, Huntington, WV

I pass a familiar park-walker who
nods *ok ok ok* as he passes the lilacs,
which start to open for business—

their job, making more.
The man doesn't bow or cringe
or side-eye me. Maybe he's crazy

lonely and imagines the No One
beside him, the gone twin,
brother, father.

He doesn't mind my quick-away look.
His hair's bright white like my dad's.
His crazy was losing hindsight;

mine is worrying foresight.
Now a bike for two wheels by,
and the boy who pedals behind says, "Byron,

why do you have to be so . . ." bipedal,
uptight, romantic? Everything
multiplies now, queries we can't

entirely hear, viruses, fears.
The No Body beside walking man
is sheer like the scent of cut grass

the wind carries across Four Pole Creek's
small rift in the world. The bike
reminds me of biplane wings, flying low,

twin daredevils, facing each other.
And the lilacs? Whitman's dooryard.
There goes the under-mind,

veering. Her path's tangential, a bit slant.
She sidles along, archetype or haint,
and goosebumps my left arm.

I wonder if dazzle-head gets that too,
no harm, no blame, just a chill beside him.

The Powers of X and the Rule of E

The electric lines' lopsided X
sways and slip-slides:
the hindleg looks to rub
spruce limbs the wind fiddles.
The sky beyond looks like snow,
my weathery husband
would say, he of the one X, one Y.

Yes, I lord it over him, complex,
with my extra legful of chromosomes:
I take my stand, arms lifted
up and out, legs splayed, unladylike
X—doubled—anonymous
Victorian porn author, or woman
of mystery, but headless, alas.

My husband would head
the household, *milord*, if it were 1604
and Elizabeth the First
hadn't finished queening and fire
still gave the light she read and wrote fiats by.
No wonder she didn't marry, cede
control to a patronym.
My confirmation name's Elizabeth.
I like to rule.

Rain jewels the wires now,
a tribute to whatever X it stands for
or against. Today I think *ex nihilo*,
from nothing, the stuff myth
says God made us from—
that and words;
or it's the hole
we're all birthed from,
mother nothing's lips,
where father thing laid seed:

we're all female
first anyway: the clitoris
turns penis. *Is, is,*
they both end:
through their pairing
we come to be.

Litany of Red

Red of the letter I,
which Amanda cut crosswise
on her wrist. High-res
and heady,

red of wound's mouth
that sang Gloria's blues,
her lament of not being
an I.

Red of Daddy's dark roses,
their scent, peppery.
Red of carnation's spice,
which Gloria

wished she were
incarnate in—she'd like
many more lips.
Red of Orphan Annie

braids, which Gloria
also wants, please, for she
is orphaned, bodiless
but for Amanda.

Red of cardinal's silhouette
at the window, one eye
showing, as he sings
his longing for a girl bird

to make more red.
Red of want,
blood and bid to join
with another,

to be and make be.
Red of sun gilding the lilac

bush, the beautiful
phallic spurs,

Whitman's and ours.
Red of the stranger's pink-red
penis exposed, one-eyed
boy, wingless, swollen—

is it sick or angry?
What beads its cyclops eye?
Ambiguous red.
Red of Daddy's

pack of Pall Malls,
a brick of death
on the pie table.
Red of the chapel's

crucifixion, the fresco's
angels in rosy cloaks:
red of rosary beads
Gloria prayed, garnets

like pomegranate seeds.
Red of stop signs,
fire engines,
red of dread and alarm.

Syncope

The circuitry's *nope*
stops the buzz supposed
to be me. I don't slip
into the photo-troping
yellow tulips that spruce up
the walkway; don't fly the leaf-scape
maples the wind cues, the clouds' nip-
and-tuck; don't seep
into Daddy's cat nap
in sun spot. I don't elope
with a dream man. I lapse,
no tropes at hand, no quips,
eclipsed like anesthesia's "Clap!
You're out!" Not rapt

but telescoped, stopped.
Time doesn't elapse:
it does a runner, a skip,
a warp-speed leap.
I'm Daddy's lost words, the lisp
of loss. I'm Penelope's dropped
stitch, the rosary's skipped
Hail Mary, the missed step

in the theorem I think I'm
more than, slam
without dunk, scam
the Buddha knows I am—
boast in a skin,
hoop without a rim.

To the Ghost of Humid Nights

You're so light, sister bird-foot, you gust
and whistle uphill and down the side I
can't quite see, where the hollow resurrects
mist. Days, the woods gather it,
the warm and humid nights set it loose,
gray-blue pearls a girl might wear or be:
sway and drape, slow dance
the ridges have mothered.
Sister who was, then wasn't, ghost story:
I've imagined you haloed and pale
like the drowned, or blooded, flush
with energy, riding air and the woods' luscious
scents, oak bark, humus, pine. Do you know
who whistled up the musk and gristle
we are? You've licked the light
off Four Pole Creek. If not flesh and bone,
gust in the mist. Earth is your mouth.

The Mask

On Pollock's *Bird Effort*

Those coils, are they birds or entrails?
They veer into or grow

inside each other: sinuous necks,
beaked and billed heads, round

bodies. The thick black outlines
don't forestall the slippage:

they insist. A duck head smiles, its eye
and brow Groucho's,

and below, the throat's other bill
opens, black lines between the halves,

and a tongue. A smaller bird lodges in another,
gray and hunched, a hawk, the eyes,

points, watching. Everything mothers another
or has eaten it. The colors are avian, jay's

and bunting's blues, vireo greens,
rooster reds, while the eider-neck teal

ground winds around. The small jade
duck sitting at the painting's foot

may float under an upside-down seagull
whose neck and eye are crimson, bill

slightly open. Is the gull bloody or just red?
I step back, and the whole coil

looks like a bird mask:
two eyes, the head made of bird

parts, and the gull caught in the beak:
the palette is preen, swim

and kill, the head a swarm
of guts, beak a mechanism

for tearing and singing:
it's nothing like me.

Amanda's Quite Contrary

Awake at six, hair gelled and spiked
by 6:05, I say my morning mantra
to mirror-me: *It's ok to be me*
ok to be me ok to be me.
I line my eyelids day-glo blue,
pull up my Levi's 505s,
loop Mother's pearls around my
crew neck T: I like
a mixed diction.

Already dressed, the downy woodpecker
works the walnut tree.
His red cap bobs up down
up down. His back's barred
black and white, decked out
like Baltimore catechism's
black and white milk bottles
illustrating the soul's states,
grace or sin.

Uncontrite, he inclines up
the branch so fast
priests can't catch him:
he's *both/and*, not
either/or, contraries married
and capped with acclaim.

He pauses, pecks beetle stock,
larval plenty, then flicks
to the next ripe spot.
Black eyes white rimmed,
he's a small spectacle
bespectacled. I like his whim
and festival.

One-footed hop,
head bob, I do my lips
downy-cap red.

Legions of Misprisions

One scissored head looks like another,
though near the mausoleum
two topiaries whose manes imply *lion*
look like moons with ruffs and ears.
My patronym is the female of them:
Loewe, the lioness. The German
sounds like the English *love*;
the American is *lowee*.
They've pruned the yews here
to lopsided cubes, the geometry
unrulier than clouds, snip-carved
a rabbit-eared horse head, an earless dog.
Legions of misprisions.

I can imagine Dad buried
near the stone angel:
she reaches up, one wing extended, longing
made into a thing.
It's a rich man's
last dominion. Dominic,
the Irish mom named him.
He dominated no one, though he
fell from a great height in his B-52
and outlived a broken skull,
riveted, the memory-bone skewed.

Nobody's topiary now,
he paid to burn and be strewn
to the sea from a yacht's prow,
the sails billowing air and light,

but he was twice burned,
scammed. His columbarium
a vacant lot, a brush fire melted
the distinctions—the plastic
urns burst, scattered man-ash,
woman-ash, self, other:
he's no one and everyone,
conflagration's anonymous son.

Not even a topiary lion
mocks his name.
This is his marker.

In Which I Almost Become Dorothy Parker

I mask up and mind the road-worker-orange
Xs Kroger marked
every six feet on the floor—
skewed crosses, shorthand
for old lovers, or algebra's dark-
horse unknowns.
We mask and glove up like debutantes
or Michael Jackson wannabes,
ever so gaunt and elegant,
and avoid eye contact
with the barefaced.
The virus I just learned
can ride air motes—
shed skin, the cat's hair,
mine, yours, my Great Aunt Julia's
studio-photo's dust—
everything's its horse.

I met Julia only once,
who commanded me to kiss
her papery cheek, who now is photograph
and erasure, fixer unfixed,
who survived the Spanish flu
and two World Wars only to disperse
in the ill air. I'm the blue-haired
lady now, masquerading,
debuting by the jams,
doing a turn at the bread aisle,
pushing the silvery chrome
grocery cart, glamorous
chariot bearing New Dawn, Raid, Lysol—
a highly recommended cocktail

that would end my tale,
Gloria's, Julia's, and whoever
else's evermore
I am the last walking memorial
of, including my x's.

I loved you all, sort of,
and words more than sex,
which I liked a lot, and my daughter
absolutely . . . and . . . I can't unlove
her, leave her that eternal
sour note, that *not*.

I'd better Lysol drawer handles,
keyboard, doorknobs.
I'll forsake nothing: masks, gloves,
aisles where the virus dances,
words, loves, daughters,
dead women poets—whoever
I bear the memory of.

That preposition I just ended on?
It points to the next noun,
the next now, that dark horse—
optimism.

The Vanished Twin Gives up Punctuation at the New River

I am knotting and
unknotting
the absences

of stops and provisos
making me fluent
so you can't distinguish
thought from thought
Amanda from
me from the river

I am the rush of
its whirls and foam
the rocks which mist me
an aura
I ride and am

while the white sun slips
the horizon
a host glossing it all

and the hidden rocks
buckle and flex my
sheer muscles
which run on
over the pink sandstone

riverbed that is
mainly Amanda

Amanda on the Angel of the Knowledge of Death

Now a warmth, then a chill, she fits me,
an underskin. When I eat the light with wide
mouth, she laughs, swallowing all
openings and passageways—doorway,
staircase, well in the churchyard. She wants
to sail and sink like flat thin stones we skip
over Ritter Park Creek, radiating zeros,
ellipses of lips. Sometimes she sits, thick
waisted, inert, practicing the elocution of rain—
its iterative mumble—for she has grown dense
with the weight of dying. Even the roadcuts
in spring pranked with violets and pink
lady's slippers are only aftermath, foreboding—
she cannot vanish entirely into ash, into ode.

Amanda, Cartographer

Most atlases show the usual
continents and oceans—the blue
a unique map shade, cerulean but dull,
as if we can't handle full-on
cobalt, indigo, turquoise. The land's
main is green, singed brown,
and some countries are inked
yellow or over-rouged-cheek pink.
I like irregular boundaries, warted,
jigsawed, and toothy like gears,
and prefer the ancient maps, weird

in the old sense, suited to dragons
flaming from caverns
and batting bat-style wings, and whales
in the sea who bear fountains like ponytails
on their heads. From one cliff, fly-sized,
winged lovers leap into tidal
pools not marked but surely called
"Oops" and "Oh no!" On a plain
nearby, miniscule persons
till and sow, and, since time and seasons
aren't things maps do, other folks may work
tiny orchards of delicious but quirky
star- and dragon-fruit, maybe some quince.

I'd prefer more *if* and less *then*
and vacationing on a continent
where balloons transport everyone,
little flames just kissing
the air over their heads—so, yes,
a few near misses.
I'd have friends with various ears, mulish
or kittenish or hound droopy, but plush
and amiable. Maybe I'd be a special
eye-animal: a basilisk
who gives up killing and asks
nothing but a good ear rub, or a gypsy
moth who likes to lisp by your lips

and brush them with the faux eyes
on her wings, or a peacock whose tail
elicits swoon and sigh—the teal
and dragonfly-blue sheen, the awful cry.

I wonder if all cartographers draw
the maps they are?

How the One Is Two, Amanda and Her Vanished Twin

after Betsy Sholl, "Genealogy"

One sister worships photons, the other adores
the Dark Knight morning glory, purple-black.

One worries God who massacred the Midianites,
the other thinks earthquakes and rogue waves divine.

One expunges herself from Facebook every night before bed,
the other splurges herself, does Insta at two a.m.

Amanda learned their ancestors came
from the steppes, Gloria thought Paris.

Gloria squanders on flat shoes, Amanda hoards
heels—read that as you will.

The one's calves are well muscled
because she loves running the park, the other prefers

drinking Miller High Life in her Chevy
and buzzing St. Joe's—scofflaw.

The awe-abiding one loves the jaw-drop of wonder
and admires thunder rolling boulders downslope.

One hears bells in the rose and bowl of her ear.
One hears the long sigh of bus exhaust.

One is a stone with one ear to the earth,
the other a bay that asterisks its own blue in the window.

One is NY, one Sonoma.
Sleeping, they dream each other.

Falling and Calling

Then they fall through you,
the small islands of sunlight the maples and oaks
release where you walk—sheer things the birds
sing and call through in the privacy
you think you are. It reminds you the jilted girl
is tucked inside. She sheds her influence
backward and forward. Watching through your eyes
the leaves balance and spill the sun for hours,
she memorizes the random shapes of falling
light. She recalls them for you like childhood
prayers as sleep forestalls—weightless,
substanceless, as she is. She is calling
and falling through you, provoking you to love.

The Atomic Woman

My husband's open guitar score
where the notes rise or fall,
wingless or one-winged,
a murder of crows;

my father's overflowing
avocado-green, dinner-plate-sized ashtray littered
with burnt-out Old Golds—
suicide's instruments;

the sequins decorating
my daughter's Red Sox
ball cap, which nick the sparks
off Four Pole Creek;

and here, the bees' cadre,
like the WWII turbo props
my father flew,
slow-buzzing the flowering dogwood,
one hightailing it to the next flowerer,
crepe myrtle:

Socrates riddled and fiddled it,
the many and the one:
the hive mind guiding a cloud
of bees all one way;
Gloria ticking in my
inner ear; the gut's flora and fauna;
atoms and spaces swarming
and shaping a woman,
even the spine's bone-ringed cord—
Kundalini, the Hindus call it,
want's own wand.

Is it all those spaces that
prickle and pierce,
that drive us to join, to be
entered or enter another
doomed cloud of atoms,
charges and urges?

Now the tree shade's
ideograms on the lawn,
one-sided man, many-armed
woman, stump man,
Shiva and Kali, are
dismembering
memory,

and yes, the inconstant
consonants, chattering
motherbirds,
the vowels' opening mouths,

fingerbones, ear bones,
this dance:
read me, rhyme me,
make me cohere.

Acknowledgments

I am most grateful to the editors and publishers of the following journals, chapbooks, and anthologies where the poems have appeared, some in slightly different versions.

Aeolian Harp Anthology: "The Vanishing Twin Does Vertigo" as "What Vertigo Is"

Birmingham Poetry Review: "*Morpho Didius*"

Catamaran: "Van Gogh's Howl"

Cider Press Review: "In the Dress of Mirrors," "To the Ghost of Humid Nights," "To the Miscarried Child"

Connotation Press: "Amanda on the Angel of the Knowledge of Death" and "Gloria, as the Jilted Girl" as "Blazon"

Ekphrastic Review: "The Mask" as "The Eye Always Describes Itself," 2021 contest finalist

Gettysburg Review: "Syncope"

McNeese Review: "Amanda, Beached Like the Sand" as "Metaphor"

Nasty Woman Poets anthology, Lost Horse Press, 2017: "Amanda and the Man Soul"

NELLE: "The Saint of Red"; "Amanda, Showing the Father," as "Showing the Father," Three Sisters Award, 2019

Nimrod: "Antheraea Polyphemus," "Chimera," "Embroidering," "Speaking the Beast," Pablo Neruda Award, second place, 2017

Poem/Memoir/Story (now *NELLE*): "Amanda and the Man Soul," "The Gone Twin, an Origin Myth"

Prairie Schooner: "*Amaryllis Belladonna*," "In Which I Almost Become Dorothy Parker," "The Powers of X and the Rule of E"

The Power of the Feminine I, anthology, Eds, Cristal Ann Cooper Rice, Donna Biffar, 2024: "Amanda Chimera" as "Chimera"

Some of these poems appeared in the chapbook *Amanda and the Man Soul*, winner, 2017 EMRYS Prize: "Amanda and the Man Soul," "Amanda Penelope," "Atomic Woman," "The Birds of Cutting," "Chimera," "Embroidering," "The Gone Twin, an Origin Myth," "Amanda's Quite Contrary," "She Liked Ike, a Rhyme Bout," "Tuesdays in Amanda," "To the Miscarried Child," "The Vanishing Twin Does Vertigo"

Also in the chapbook *Eating the Light*, Sable Books' 2016 award: "Amanda, Beached Like the Sand" as "Metaphor" and "Light Lures"

In addition, I offer sincere thanks to the village of poets who have midwifed the poems and the book: Art Stringer, Bob Hill, Susan Kelly DeWitt, Lise Goett, Jessica Jacobs, Frank Paino, Robert Carr, Claire Bateman, Neil Shepard.

Notes

"*Antheraea Polyphemus.*" The Latin name, and some features of anatomy derive from internet sources.

"*Morpho Didius.*" A pair of Morphos came to my attention as a wedding present. Their "colours are not a result of pigmentation but rather are an example of iridescence... the ventral side is decorated with *ocelli* or eyespots." They are native to Peru. Whether they appeared in Renaissance *wunderkabinets* is my conjecture.
https://animalcorner.co.uk/animals/morpho-butterfly

"Blazon, 'Figure of a Winged Monster.'" The winged monster appears on the cover of Janis Pallister's 1982 translation of Ambroise Pare's *On Monsters and Marvels* and as an illustration in Pare's 1573 original.

"Saviors." "Sanguine" is both a color and a mood.

"Speaking the Beast." "The manticore... is the size of a lion, and is red like cinnabar: It has three rows of teeth, human ears and light blue eyes like a man's." In "Rejecting and Embracing the Monsters in Ancient Greece and Rome." D. Felton. Ed. Asa Simon Mittman and Peter J. Dendle. *The Ashgate Research Companion to Monsters and the Monstrous*, 2017.

About the Author

Mary B. Moore's published books include *Dear If*, Orison Books, 2022; *Flicker*, Dogfish Head Award, 2016; *The Book of Snow*, Cleveland State U Poetry Center, 1998; and the prize-winning chapbooks *Amanda and the Man Soul*, 2017, and *Eating the Light*, 2016. Poems appear lately in *Birmingham Poetry Review*, *POETRY*, *South Dakota Review*, *Tahoma Literary Review*, *Nimrod*, *Prairie Schooner*, *NELLE*, *Terrain*, *Catamaran*, *Calyx*, *Still: The Journal*, *Crosswinds*, and more. She has won *NELLE*'s Three Sisters Prize, *Birmingham Poetry Review*'s Collins Prize, and the second-place award in *Nimrod*'s 2017 Pablo Neruda Prize. She is a native Californian and was a professor at Marshall University in Huntington, West Virginia, where she now lives.

www.ingramcontent.com/pod-product-compliance
Lightning Source LLC
Chambersburg PA
CBHW021407090426
42742CB00009B/1048